WITHDRAWN

J
232
Gal

Galbreath, Naomi
    The story of Passover
for children

MAR 1 7 1990	DATE DUE		
AUG 2 8 1991	OCT 2 0 1995	APR 0 4 2005	
APR 2 9 1992	6-14-96	APR 0 5 2006	
JUL 2 9 1992	MAR 1 8 1995	MAR 1 0 2009	
MAR 2 7 1993	SEP 0 9 1996		
JUN 0 3 1993	MAR 1 4 1996		
7-7-93	FEB 2 6 2001		
AUG 0 3 1993	MAY 2 3 2001		
SEP 2 8 1993	JUL 3 1 2001		
3/28/94	JAN 1 8 2002		
JAN 1 8 1995			
APR 1 7 1995	APR 1 4 2004		

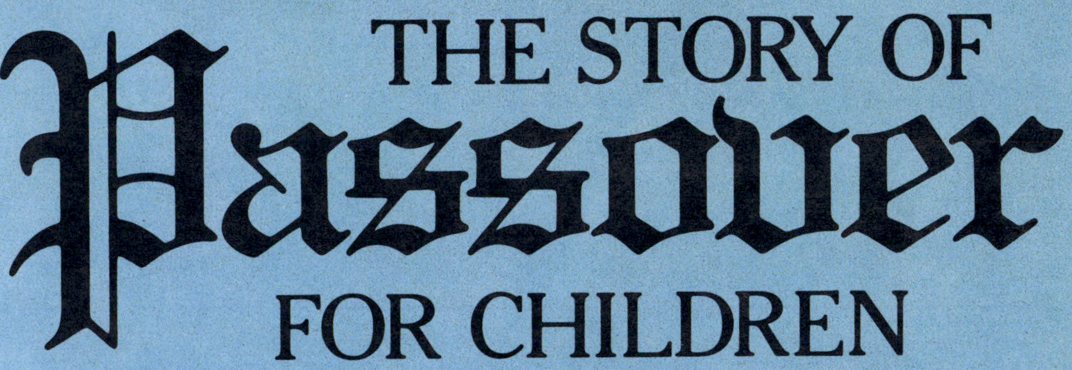

THE STORY OF Passover FOR CHILDREN

Written by
Naomi Galbreath

Illustrated by
Kurt Avdek

ideals®

CHILDRENS PRESS, CHICAGO
School & Library Edition

Copyright © MCMLXXXIV by Ideals Publishing Corporation
All rights reserved. Printed and bound in U.S.A.
Published simultaneously in Canada.

ISBN 0-516-09197-2

In distant past, in Bible times,
Enslaved by Egypt's rule,
Jews hoped to have their freedom,
For Pharaoh's tasks were cruel.

But though he heaped task upon task,
The Jews were strong and proud.
So Pharaoh was afraid, and said,
"Such strength is not allowed!"

"We'll kill their every first-born son!"
But one child, safe in water
Was hidden by his mother
And then found by Pharaoh's daughter.

She raised the boy, named Moses,
As a prince. When he was grown,
He saw his people still enslaved
With no land of their own.

And then God spoke to Moses
From within a bush of flame.
"Go to Egypt's Pharaoh! Tell him
You speak in my name."

Moses and his brother spoke
The words of God's decree
To Pharaoh: "Let my people go —
My people must be free."

"No!" Pharaoh said, "They'll stay and make
My bricks of straw and mud."
And Moses said, "Then God will turn
The rivers into blood!"

The fishes died, the river stank;
All throats were parched and dry.
Seven days of blood — the whole land rang
With Egypt's mournful cry.

"Now let us go," warned Moses,
"Or next, frogs will swarm the land —
Frogs in your beds, your ovens, clothes —
Frogs on every hand!"

The plague of frogs changed Pharaoh's mind.
"Just take these frogs away,
And you and all of Israel
Can leave this very day!"

But when the frogs were gone
The Pharaoh changed his mind again.
So God sent lice to plague
Egyptian women, children, men.

But Pharaoh's heart was hardened,
And he wouldn't let them go.
So God sent flies to swarm the land.
But Pharaoh still said no.

Moses said, "Free us — or else God
Will slay your flocks and herds.
But Israel's flocks will live."
All was according to his words.

And next appeared a plague of sores
On each Egyptian's skin.
And then a rain of hail beat down
The fields and all therein.

Next, locusts came and ate the crops
And every crust of bread.
"We'll soon have no more food!"
The Egyptians, frightened, said.

Then Pharaoh said, "I'll let you go."
And again he changed his mind.
Then Moses said, "Next God will send
Plagues of another kind."

Then God sent darkness to the land,
And day was dark as night.
Three days Egyptians dwelt in dark
While Israel dwelt in light.

The last plague was the worst of all:
Each firstborn child would die
In each Egyptian family —
And Pharaoh would know why.

But first God spoke to Moses,
Saying, "Tell your people now
To prepare to flee from Egypt —
I will tell them how.

"At the front door of every house
With lamb's blood make a mark.
Then roast the lamb and eat —
And stay in after dark."

At midnight in each Egyptian house
Every first-born died.
But God passed over Jewish homes —
The lamb's blood was his guide.

"Go!" Pharaoh said to Moses, "Go!
Or soon we'll all be dead!"
Then Moses told his people, "Take your
Herds, and dough for bread.

"Don't wait for it to rise; just run!"
With gifts of Egyptian gold
They fled the land to serve the Lord,
And as God had foretold,

Pharaoh changed his mind and chased the Jews
And was drowned in the Red Sea.
But God kept Israel's children safe.
At last they all were free.

And still today, the tale is told
Of the works that God did then,
In a Passover celebration
Which has meaning for all men.

Jews tell this tale of freedom
On Passover, in the spring.
In joyous celebration,
They feast and pray and sing.

The house is cleaned and freshened up;
Leavened bread is thrown away.
All is readied for a special meal
To begin at close of day.

At the Passover feast, the Seder,
Special foods help us recall
Those days — roast lamb and hard-boiled eggs
And flat matzah most of all.

The roasted lamb reminds us of
The door marked with lamb's blood;
Haroseth — apples, nuts, and wine —
Tells of bricks and clay and mud.

There are bitter herbs for slavery,
And blood-red wine for prayer,
Salt water for slave's bitter tears
In Egypt, or anywhere.

The hard-boiled egg is sacrifice;
The matzah is the bread
That was baked flat, for lack of time —
The Jews made it as they fled.

This is the tale the Bible tells
Of the flight from Egypt's land,
Of God, his many mighty works,
And of Moses and his stand.

Year after year the tale was told
In the house of every Jew.
The parents taught their children
And their children's children, too.

Years passed. A Jew from Nazareth,
A carpenter, broke bread
With friends at his last supper
When Passover prayers were said.

His name was Jesus, and he knew
The meaning of the feast —
That God had shown his goodness;
Men from bondage were released.

Grandfather gives the blessing,
And then the youngest son
Asks the four Passover questions;
The story is begun.

Grandfather reads from the Haggadah,
A very special book
That tells about the struggle
That gaining freedom took.

The family has invited
Guests and strangers without kin.
A glass of wine, an open door
Welcome prophet Elijah in.

A piece of matzah's hidden
Which the children hunt to find
For a reward — they look everywhere!
No one seems to mind.

With songs of hope, with songs of praise —
The whole room fills with song!
Old songs sung every Seder night
By voices glad and strong.

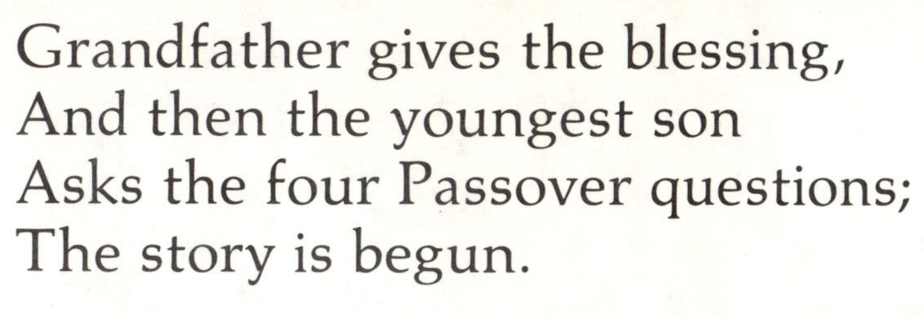

On Passover, Jews and Christians both
Bring these events to mind
Which show how God brings freedom —
Freedom for all mankind.